This book belongs to

_____

For Kim Menzel Myer,
my lifelong friend.

One to Grow On™
Bible Series

My Bible Colors

Written by
Tracy Harrast

Illustrated by
Nancy Munger

Zondervan Publishing House
Grand Rapids, Michigan

God Looks at the Heart

Some people may notice
If we're big or we're small,
What color our skin is,
If we're short or we're tall.

But God sees us differently.
He is loving and smart.
When God looks at us,
He looks at our heart.

Red Heart

But the LORD said to Samuel, "Do not consider how handsome or tall he is . . . I do not look at the things people look at. Man looks at how someone appears on the outside. But I look at what is in the heart" (1 Samuel 16:7).

Like a Tree by Water

A tree near water has what it needs.
Its roots drink where water is flowing.
Even when days are hot and dry,
Its green leaves keep right on growing.

If we stay close to God *we* will grow too,
Like a tree with its roots by a stream.
God's love will always keep us strong,
No matter how big troubles seem.

Green Leaves

But I will bless any man who trusts in me ... He will be like a tree that is planted near water. It sends out its roots beside a stream. It is not afraid when heat comes. Its leaves are always green ... It always bears fruit (Jeremiah 17:7–8).

Jesus Walks on Water

Jesus walked on the water
To reach his friends in a boat.
Peter asked to try it too.
And at first he started to float!

But Peter was scared by the wind
    and waves
And because he was far from shore.
He began to sink but was saved
    by Jesus,
Who told Peter to trust him more.

Blue Water

Early in the morning, Jesus went out to the disciples. He walked on the lake (Matthew 14:25).

Before the Sunset

The bright yellow sun
  In a sky that's clear blue
    Reminds us of something
    God wants us to do.

  When we feel angry,
  Forgive and forget.
  Get over it quickly,
  Before the sunset.

When you are angry, do not sin (Psalm 4:4). Do not let the sun go down while you are still angry (Ephesians 4:26).

Finding What's Lost

A lady with ten silver coins lost one,
So she looked and looked all around.
She lit a lamp and swept the floor.
She searched until it was found.

She threw a party to celebrate—
She had her coin back again!
God feels happy like that too
When sinners turn from their sin.

Silver Coin

Suppose a woman has ten silver coins and loses one. She will light a lamp and sweep the house. She will search carefully until she finds the coin. And when she finds it, she will call her friends and neighbors together. She will say, "Be joyful with me. I have found my lost coin." . . . It is the same in heaven. There is joy in heaven over one sinner who turns away from sin (Luke 15:8–10).

The Rich Man and the Poor Man

A rich man wore fine purple clothes
And wouldn't share food from his plate.
He did nothing to help poor Lazarus,
Who was hungry and begged at his gate.

The poor man died and went to heaven,
Where he was forever glad.
But when the rich man died
He was forever sad.

Purple Clothes

Once there was a rich man. He was dressed in purple cloth and fine linen. He lived an easy life every day. A man named Lazarus was placed at his gate. Lazarus was a beggar (Luke 16:19–20).

A Burning Bush

One day on a mountain
As Moses was walking,
He saw a bush burning
And heard the Lord talking.

God's people in Egypt
Had cried out in prayer.
God heard and told Moses,
"Go get them from there!"

Orange Fire

Moses saw that the bush was on fire. But it didn't burn up ... God spoke to him from inside the bush. He called out, "Moses! Moses!" "Here I am," Moses said. The LORD said, "I have seen my people suffer in Egypt. I have heard them cry out ... I want you to bring the Israelites out of Egypt" (Exodus 3:2, 4, 7, 10).

Jesus Stops a Storm

Gray storm clouds rolled right in,
Dropping rain and flashing lightning.
Friends of Jesus in a boat
Thought the storm was very
frightening.

They begged Jesus to help them
and not let them drown.
Jesus told the storm, "Quiet!"
and calmed it right down.

Gray Clouds

[Jesus] got up and ordered the wind to stop. He said to the waves, "Quiet! Be still!" Then the wind died down. And it was completely calm (Mark 4:39).

A Family Too Big to Count

An angel came to tell Abraham
A blessing God had planned:
His family would have as many kids
As there are grains of sand.

More children than we can count
Are in Abraham's family today.
We think of this story at the beach
And in the sandbox when we play.

Tan Sand

I will certainly bless you. I will make your children after you as many as the stars in the sky. I will make them as many as the grains of sand on the seashore (Genesis 22:17).

God Sends Birds With Food

A man named Elijah
Had nothing to eat.
    He was very hungry
    For bread and for meat.

God knew Elijah's needs,
And he heard him pray.
    So God sent big black birds
    To bring food twice a day.

Black Bird

*So Elijah did what the L*ORD *had told him to do . . . The ravens brought him bread and meat in the morning. They also brought him bread and meat in the evening. He drank water from the brook* (1 Kings 17:5–6).

Why Jesus Died for Us

Jesus gave up his life
On a cross that was brown.
He said, "It is finished."
And he put his head down.

On a cross that was brown
On a very sad day,
Jesus died so our sins
Could be taken away.

Brown Cross

They nailed Jesus to the cross. Two other men were crucified with him. One was on each side of him. Jesus was in the middle ... After Jesus drank he said, "It is finished." Then he bowed his head and died (John 19:18, 30). *He gave his life to pay for our sins* (1 John 2:2).

An Angel at the Tomb

At Jesus' tomb, his friends saw an angel.
Like lightning, the angel was bright.
He sat on the stone he had rolled away.
His clothes were pure, sparkling white.

The angel had some news for them
That changed their lives for good:
"Jesus isn't here. He's risen,
Just as he said he would!"

Angel in White

There was a powerful earthquake. An angel of the Lord came down from heaven. The angel went to the tomb. He rolled back the stone and sat on it. His body shone like lightning. His clothes were as white as snow. The angel said to the women "[Jesus] is not here! He has risen, just as he said he would . . . " (Matthew 28:2–3, 5–6).

Where God Lives

There are no sad tears in heaven.
No one gets sick or grows old.
The sea is clear there, like crystal.
The main street is made from pure
    gold!

All of us in heaven will be happy.
We'll sing and we'll never be bored.
But the very best part about heaven
Is that we'll get to be with our Lord!

Gold Street

There will be no more death or sadness. There will be no more crying or pain ... The main street of the city was made out of pure gold, as clear as glass (Revelation 21:4, 21).

What Colors Do You See?

Joseph was given a beautiful coat
By Israel, his loving dad.
Can you name all of the colors
  That Joseph's bright coat may
    have had?

  Where are yellow and tan and gray?
Do you see white, green, and blue?
Can you find orange, black, and purple?
Point to brown, red, and gold too.

Colorful Coat

Israel loved Joseph more than any of his other sons . . . Israel made him a beautiful robe (Genesis 37:3).

Author: Tracy Harrast
Illustrator: Nancy Munger
Project Management and Editorial: Catherine DeVries
Interior Design: Sue Vandenberg Koppenol
Art Direction and Cover Direction: Jody Langley